ISBN

  Wire-O Softcover: 978-1-957029-12-2

  Softcover / Paperback: 978-1-957029-13-9

DEDICATION

This book is dedicated to all those who seek restoration.

January, 20____

During this month, do your best to memorize this verse.

Come to me,
all you who are weary and burdened,
and I will give you rest.
(Matthew 11:28, NIV)

Write your featured month verse here. Dissect the verse and re-write it using your own words. Doodle the verse. Print it. Repeat it as often as possible.

_____

_____

_____

_____

_____

_____

_____

_____

_____

_____

_____

_____

_____

_____

_____

_____

_____

_____

_____

✳ *Personal* ✳

My Thanksgiving... _____
_____
_____

My Repentance... _____
_____
_____

My Needs... _____
_____
_____

My Worries... _____
_____
_____

My Desires... _____
_____
_____

Who I need to forgive... _____
_____
_____

✳ *My Family* ✳

Family Name: _____

Concern: _____

Date Answered: _____

Family Name: _____

Concern: _____

Date Answered: _____

Family Name: _____

Concern: _____

Date Answered: _____

Family Name: _____

Concern: _____

Date Answered: _____

Family Name: _____

Concern: _____

Date Answered: _____

Family Name: _____

Concern: _____

Date Answered: _____

Family Name: _____

Concern: _____

Date Answered: _____

Family Name: _____

Concern: _____

Date Answered: _____

Family Name: _____

Concern: _____

Date Answered: _____

Family Name: _____

Concern: _____

Date Answered: _____

✳ *My Friends* ✳

Friend's Name: _____   Friend's Name: _____

Concern: _____   Concern: _____

Date Answered: _____   Date Answered: _____

Friend's Name: _____   Friend's Name: _____

Concern: _____   Concern: _____

Date Answered: _____   Date Answered: _____

Friend's Name: _____   Friend's Name: _____

Concern: _____   Concern: _____

Date Answered: _____   Date Answered: _____

Friend's Name: _____   Friend's Name: _____

Concern: _____   Concern: _____

Date Answered: _____   Date Answered: _____

Friend's Name: _____   Friend's Name: _____

Concern: _____   Concern: _____

Date Answered: _____   Date Answered: _____

✳ Prayers Requested by Others ✳

Name: _____   Name: _____

Concern: _____   Concern: _____

Date Answered: _____   Date Answered: _____

Name: _____   Name: _____

Concern: _____   Concern: _____

Date Answered: _____   Date Answered: _____

Name: _____   Name: _____

Concern: _____   Concern: _____

Date Answered: _____   Date Answered: _____

Name: _____   Name: _____

Concern: _____   Concern: _____

Date Answered: _____   Date Answered: _____

Name: _____   Name: _____

Concern: _____   Concern: _____

Date Answered: _____   Date Answered: _____

✳ *Scribble your thoughts...* ✳

Come
you who
are weary.

Find
rest.

February, 20___ ___

During this month, do your best to memorize this verse.

Do not conform to the pattern of this world,
but be transformed by the renewing of your mind.
Then you will be able to test and approve what
God's will is—his good, pleasing and perfect will.
(Romans 12:2, NIV)

Write your featured month verse here. Dissect the verse
and re-write it using your own words. Doodle the verse.
Print it. Repeat it as often as possible.

_____

_____

_____

_____

_____

_____

_____

_____

_____

_____

_____

_____

_____

_____

✳ Personal ✳

My Thanksgiving... _____

_____

_____

My Repentance... _____

_____

_____

My Needs... _____

_____

_____

My Worries... _____

_____

_____

My Desires... _____

_____

_____

Who I need to forgive... _____

_____

_____

✳ My Family ✳

Family Name: _____

Concern: _____

Date Answered: _____

Family Name: _____

Concern: _____

Date Answered: _____

Family Name: _____

Concern: _____

Date Answered: _____

Family Name: _____

Concern: _____

Date Answered: _____

Family Name: _____

Concern: _____

Date Answered: _____

Family Name: _____

Concern: _____

Date Answered: _____

Family Name: _____

Concern: _____

Date Answered: _____

Family Name: _____

Concern: _____

Date Answered: _____

Family Name: _____

Concern: _____

Date Answered: _____

Family Name: _____

Concern: _____

Date Answered: _____

✳ *My Friends* ✳

Friend's Name: _____

Concern: _____

Date Answered: _____

Friend's Name: _____

Concern: _____

Date Answered: _____

Friend's Name: _____

Concern: _____

Date Answered: _____

Friend's Name: _____

Concern: _____

Date Answered: _____

Friend's Name: _____

Concern: _____

Date Answered: _____

Friend's Name: _____

Concern: _____

Date Answered: _____

Friend's Name: _____

Concern: _____

Date Answered: _____

Friend's Name: _____

Concern: _____

Date Answered: _____

Friend's Name: _____

Concern: _____

Date Answered: _____

Friend's Name: _____

Concern: _____

Date Answered: _____

☀ Prayers Requested by Others ☀

Name: _____

Concern: _____

Date Answered: _____

Name: _____

Concern: _____

Date Answered: _____

Name: _____

Concern: _____

Date Answered: _____

Name: _____

Concern: _____

Date Answered: _____

Name: _____

Concern: _____

Date Answered: _____

Name: _____

Concern: _____

Date Answered: _____

Name: _____

Concern: _____

Date Answered: _____

Name: _____

Concern: _____

Date Answered: _____

Name: _____

Concern: _____

Date Answered: _____

Name: _____

Concern: _____

Date Answered: _____

✳ *Scribble your thoughts...* ✳

DO NOT CONFORM TO THE PATTERN OF THIS WORLD

BE Transformed!

March, 20___ ___

During this month, do your best to memorize this verse.

And the God of all grace,
who called you to his eternal glory in Christ,
after you have suffered a little while,
will himself restore you
and make you strong, firm and steadfast.
To him be the power for ever and ever. Amen.
(1 Peter 5:10-11, NIV)

Write your featured month verse here. Dissect the verse and re-write it using your own words. Doodle the verse. Print it. Repeat it as often as possible.

_____

_____

_____

_____

_____

_____

_____

_____

_____

_____

_____

_____

_____

_____

_____

✳ *Personal* ✳

My Thanksgiving... _____

_____

_____

My Repentance... _____

_____

_____

My Needs... _____

_____

_____

My Worries... _____

_____

_____

My Desires... _____

_____

_____

Who I need to forgive... _____

_____

_____

✳ *My Family* ✳

Family Name: _____   Family Name: _____

Concern: _____   Concern: _____

Date Answered: _____   Date Answered: _____

Family Name: _____   Family Name: _____

Concern: _____   Concern: _____

Date Answered: _____   Date Answered: _____

Family Name: _____   Family Name: _____

Concern: _____   Concern: _____

Date Answered: _____   Date Answered: _____

Family Name: _____   Family Name: _____

Concern: _____   Concern: _____

Date Answered: _____   Date Answered: _____

Family Name: _____   Family Name: _____

Concern: _____   Concern: _____

Date Answered: _____   Date Answered: _____

✳ *My Friends* ✳

Friend's Name: _____   Friend's Name: _____

Concern: _____   Concern: _____

Date Answered: _____   Date Answered: _____

Friend's Name: _____   Friend's Name: _____

Concern: _____   Concern: _____

Date Answered: _____   Date Answered: _____

Friend's Name: _____   Friend's Name: _____

Concern: _____   Concern: _____

Date Answered: _____   Date Answered: _____

Friend's Name: _____   Friend's Name: _____

Concern: _____   Concern: _____

Date Answered: _____   Date Answered: _____

Friend's Name: _____   Friend's Name: _____

Concern: _____   Concern: _____

Date Answered: _____   Date Answered: _____

✳ Prayers Requested by Others ✳

Name: _____   Name: _____

Concern: _____   Concern: _____

Date Answered: _____   Date Answered: _____

Name: _____   Name: _____

Concern: _____   Concern: _____

Date Answered: _____   Date Answered: _____

Name: _____   Name: _____

Concern: _____   Concern: _____

Date Answered: _____   Date Answered: _____

Name: _____   Name: _____

Concern: _____   Concern: _____

Date Answered: _____   Date Answered: _____

Name: _____   Name: _____

Concern: _____   Concern: _____

Date Answered: _____   Date Answered: _____

Scribble your thoughts... *

He
himself
will restore you.
Strong. Firm.
Steadfast!

April, 20___ ___

During this month, do your best to memorize this verse.

If you, Lord, kept a record of sins,
Lord, who could stand?
But with you there is forgiveness,
so that we can, with reverence, serve you.
(Psalm 130: 3-4, NIV)

Write your featured month verse here. Dissect the verse
and re-write it using your own words. Doodle the verse.
Print it. Repeat it as often as possible.

_____

_____

_____

_____

_____

_____

_____

_____

_____

_____

_____

_____

_____

_____

✳ *Personal* ✳

My Thanksgiving... _____
_____
_____

My Repentance... _____
_____
_____

My Needs... _____
_____
_____

My Worries... _____
_____
_____

My Desires... _____
_____
_____

Who I need to forgive... _____
_____
_____

✳ My Family ✳

Family Name: _____

Concern: _____

Date Answered: _____

Family Name: _____

Concern: _____

Date Answered: _____

Family Name: _____

Concern: _____

Date Answered: _____

Family Name: _____

Concern: _____

Date Answered: _____

Family Name: _____

Concern: _____

Date Answered: _____

Family Name: _____

Concern: _____

Date Answered: _____

Family Name: _____

Concern: _____

Date Answered: _____

Family Name: _____

Concern: _____

Date Answered: _____

Family Name: _____

Concern: _____

Date Answered: _____

Family Name: _____

Concern: _____

Date Answered: _____

✳ My Friends ✳

Friend's Name: _____

Concern: _____

Date Answered: _____

Friend's Name: _____

Concern: _____

Date Answered: _____

Friend's Name: _____

Concern: _____

Date Answered: _____

Friend's Name: _____

Concern: _____

Date Answered: _____

Friend's Name: _____

Concern: _____

Date Answered: _____

Friend's Name: _____

Concern: _____

Date Answered: _____

Friend's Name: _____

Concern: _____

Date Answered: _____

Friend's Name: _____

Concern: _____

Date Answered: _____

Friend's Name: _____

Concern: _____

Date Answered: _____

Friend's Name: _____

Concern: _____

Date Answered: _____

✳ Prayers Requested by Others ✳

Name: _____

Concern: _____

Date Answered: _____

Name: _____

Concern: _____

Date Answered: _____

Name: _____

Concern: _____

Date Answered: _____

Name: _____

Concern: _____

Date Answered: _____

Name: _____

Concern: _____

Date Answered: _____

Name: _____

Concern: _____

Date Answered: _____

Name: _____

Concern: _____

Date Answered: _____

Name: _____

Concern: _____

Date Answered: _____

Name: _____

Concern: _____

Date Answered: _____

Name: _____

Concern: _____

Date Answered: _____

✳ *Scribble your thoughts...* ✳

Forgiven !

May, 20___

During this month, do your best to memorize this verse.

In the same way, the Spirit helps us in our weakness.
We do not know what we ought to pray for,
but the Spirit himself intercedes for us
through wordless groans.
(Romans 8: 26 NIV)

Write your featured month verse here. Dissect the verse and re-write it using your own words. Doodle the verse. Print it. Repeat it as often as possible.

_____
_____
_____
_____
_____
_____
_____
_____
_____
_____
_____
_____
_____
_____
_____
_____

✳ Personal ✳

My Thanksgiving... _____
_____
_____

My Repentance... _____
_____
_____

My Needs... _____
_____
_____

My Worries... _____
_____
_____

My Desires... _____
_____
_____

Who I need to forgive... _____
_____
_____

✴ My Family ✴

Family Name: _____

Concern: _____

Date Answered: _____

Family Name: _____

Concern: _____

Date Answered: _____

Family Name: _____

Concern: _____

Date Answered: _____

Family Name: _____

Concern: _____

Date Answered: _____

Family Name: _____

Concern: _____

Date Answered: _____

Family Name: _____

Concern: _____

Date Answered: _____

Family Name: _____

Concern: _____

Date Answered: _____

Family Name: _____

Concern: _____

Date Answered: _____

Family Name: _____

Concern: _____

Date Answered: _____

Family Name: _____

Concern: _____

Date Answered: _____

✳ *My Friends* ✳

Friend's Name: _____

Concern: _____

Date Answered: _____

Friend's Name: _____

Concern: _____

Date Answered: _____

Friend's Name: _____

Concern: _____

Date Answered: _____

Friend's Name: _____

Concern: _____

Date Answered: _____

Friend's Name: _____

Concern: _____

Date Answered: _____

Friend's Name: _____

Concern: _____

Date Answered: _____

Friend's Name: _____

Concern: _____

Date Answered: _____

Friend's Name: _____

Concern: _____

Date Answered: _____

Friend's Name: _____

Concern: _____

Date Answered: _____

Friend's Name: _____

Concern: _____

Date Answered: _____

✳ *Prayers Requested by Others* ✳

Name: _____   Name: _____

Concern: _____   Concern: _____

Date Answered: _____   Date Answered: _____

Name: _____   Name: _____

Concern: _____   Concern: _____

Date Answered: _____   Date Answered: _____

Name: _____   Name: _____

Concern: _____   Concern: _____

Date Answered: _____   Date Answered: _____

Name: _____   Name: _____

Concern: _____   Concern: _____

Date Answered: _____   Date Answered: _____

Name: _____   Name: _____

Concern: _____   Concern: _____

Date Answered: _____   Date Answered: _____

✶ Scribble your thoughts... ✶

The Spirit intercedes.

June, 20__ __
During this month, do your best to memorize this verse.

*You see at just the right time, when we were
still powerless, Christ died for the ungodly.
But God demonstrates his own love for us in this:
While we were still sinners, Christ died for us.
(Romans 5: 6, 8 NIV)*

Write your featured month verse here. Dissect the verse and re-write it using your own words. Doodle the verse. Print it. Repeat it as often as possible.

_____

_____

_____

_____

_____

_____

_____

_____

_____

_____

_____

_____

_____

_____

_____

_____

✴ Personal ✴

My Thanksgiving... _____

_____

_____

My Repentance... _____

_____

_____

My Needs... _____

_____

_____

My Worries... _____

_____

_____

My Desires... _____

_____

_____

Who I need to forgive... _____

_____

_____

✳ *My Family* ✳

Family Name: _____

Concern: _____

Date Answered: _____

Family Name: _____

Concern: _____

Date Answered: _____

Family Name: _____

Concern: _____

Date Answered: _____

Family Name: _____

Concern: _____

Date Answered: _____

Family Name: _____

Concern: _____

Date Answered: _____

Family Name: _____

Concern: _____

Date Answered: _____

Family Name: _____

Concern: _____

Date Answered: _____

Family Name: _____

Concern: _____

Date Answered: _____

Family Name: _____

Concern: _____

Date Answered: _____

Family Name: _____

Concern: _____

Date Answered: _____

✳ *My Friends* ✳

Friend's Name: _____   Friend's Name: _____

Concern: _____   Concern: _____

Date Answered: _____   Date Answered: _____

Friend's Name: _____   Friend's Name: _____

Concern: _____   Concern: _____

Date Answered: _____   Date Answered: _____

Friend's Name: _____   Friend's Name: _____

Concern: _____   Concern: _____

Date Answered: _____   Date Answered: _____

Friend's Name: _____   Friend's Name: _____

Concern: _____   Concern: _____

Date Answered: _____   Date Answered: _____

Friend's Name: _____   Friend's Name: _____

Concern: _____   Concern: _____

Date Answered: _____   Date Answered: _____

✳ *Prayers Requested by Others* ✳

Name: _____   Name: _____

Concern: _____   Concern: _____

Date Answered: _____   Date Answered: _____

Name: _____   Name: _____

Concern: _____   Concern: _____

Date Answered: _____   Date Answered: _____

Name: _____   Name: _____

Concern: _____   Concern: _____

Date Answered: _____   Date Answered: _____

Name: _____   Name: _____

Concern: _____   Concern: _____

Date Answered: _____   Date Answered: _____

Name: _____   Name: _____

Concern: _____   Concern: _____

Date Answered: _____   Date Answered: _____

✳ *Scribble your thoughts...* ✳

To show   His
love,
While we were
still sinners, Jesus
died for
us.

July, 20___ ___

During this month, do your best to memorize this verse.

Restore to me the joy of your salvation
and grant me a willing spirit, to sustain me.
(Psalm 51:12, NIV)

Write your featured month verse here. Dissect the verse
and re-write it using your own words. Doodle the verse.
Print it. Repeat it as often as possible.

_____

_____

_____

_____

_____

_____

_____

_____

_____

_____

_____

_____

_____

_____

✳ *Personal* ✳

My Thanksgiving... _____
_____
_____

My Repentance... _____
_____
_____

My Needs... _____
_____
_____

My Worries... _____
_____
_____

My Desires... _____
_____
_____

Who I need to forgive... _____
_____
_____

✳ *My Family* ✳

Family Name: _____   Family Name: _____

Concern: _____   Concern: _____

Date Answered: _____   Date Answered: _____

Family Name: _____   Family Name: _____

Concern: _____   Concern: _____

Date Answered: _____   Date Answered: _____

Family Name: _____   Family Name: _____

Concern: _____   Concern: _____

Date Answered: _____   Date Answered: _____

Family Name: _____   Family Name: _____

Concern: _____   Concern: _____

Date Answered: _____   Date Answered: _____

Family Name: _____   Family Name: _____

Concern: _____   Concern: _____

Date Answered: _____   Date Answered: _____

✳ *My Friends* ✳

Friend's Name: _____   Friend's Name: _____

Concern: _____   Concern: _____

Date Answered: _____   Date Answered: _____

Friend's Name: _____   Friend's Name: _____

Concern: _____   Concern: _____

Date Answered: _____   Date Answered: _____

Friend's Name: _____   Friend's Name: _____

Concern: _____   Concern: _____

Date Answered: _____   Date Answered: _____

Friend's Name: _____   Friend's Name: _____

Concern: _____   Concern: _____

Date Answered: _____   Date Answered: _____

Friend's Name: _____   Friend's Name: _____

Concern: _____   Concern: _____

Date Answered: _____   Date Answered: _____

✳ *Prayers Requested by Others* ✳

Name: _____   Name: _____

Concern: _____   Concern: _____

Date Answered: _____   Date Answered: _____

Name: _____   Name: _____

Concern: _____   Concern: _____

Date Answered: _____   Date Answered: _____

Name: _____   Name: _____

Concern: _____   Concern: _____

Date Answered: _____   Date Answered: _____

Name: _____   Name: _____

Concern: _____   Concern: _____

Date Answered: _____   Date Answered: _____

Name: _____   Name: _____

Concern: _____   Concern: _____

Date Answered: _____   Date Answered: _____

✳ *Scribble your thoughts...* ✳

Restore
to me the

Joy
of your
salvation
oh Lord!

August, 20____

During this month, do your best to memorize this verse.

Finally, brothers and sisters, whatever is true, whatever is noble, whatever is right, whatever is pure, whatever is lovely, whatever is admirable —if anything is excellent or praiseworthy —think about such things. (Philippians 4:8, NIV)

Write your featured month verse here. Dissect the verse and re-write it using your own words. Doodle the verse. Print it. Repeat it as often as possible.

_____

_____

_____

_____

_____

_____

_____

_____

_____

_____

_____

_____

_____

_____

✴ Personal ✴

My Thanksgiving... _____
_____
_____

My Repentance... _____
_____
_____

My Needs... _____
_____
_____

My Worries... _____
_____
_____

My Desires... _____
_____
_____

Who I need to forgive... _____
_____
_____

✳ My Family ✳

Family Name: _____

Concern: _____

Date Answered: _____

Family Name: _____

Concern: _____

Date Answered: _____

Family Name: _____

Concern: _____

Date Answered: _____

Family Name: _____

Concern: _____

Date Answered: _____

Family Name: _____

Concern: _____

Date Answered: _____

Family Name: _____

Concern: _____

Date Answered: _____

Family Name: _____

Concern: _____

Date Answered: _____

Family Name: _____

Concern: _____

Date Answered: _____

Family Name: _____

Concern: _____

Date Answered: _____

Family Name: _____

Concern: _____

Date Answered: _____

✳ *My Friends* ✳

Friend's Name: _____   Friend's Name: _____

Concern: _____   Concern: _____

Date Answered: _____   Date Answered: _____

Friend's Name: _____   Friend's Name: _____

Concern: _____   Concern: _____

Date Answered: _____   Date Answered: _____

Friend's Name: _____   Friend's Name: _____

Concern: _____   Concern: _____

Date Answered: _____   Date Answered: _____

Friend's Name: _____   Friend's Name: _____

Concern: _____   Concern: _____

Date Answered: _____   Date Answered: _____

Friend's Name: _____   Friend's Name: _____

Concern: _____   Concern: _____

Date Answered: _____   Date Answered: _____

✳ Prayers Requested by Others ✳

Name: _____   Name: _____

Concern: _____   Concern: _____

Date Answered: _____   Date Answered: _____

Name: _____   Name: _____

Concern: _____   Concern: _____

Date Answered: _____   Date Answered: _____

Name: _____   Name: _____

Concern: _____   Concern: _____

Date Answered: _____   Date Answered: _____

Name: _____   Name: _____

Concern: _____   Concern: _____

Date Answered: _____   Date Answered: _____

Name: _____   Name: _____

Concern: _____   Concern: _____

Date Answered: _____   Date Answered: _____

✴ *Scribble your thoughts...* ✴

Think wonderful thoughts!

September, 20____
During this month, do your best to memorize this verse.

I waited patiently for the Lord; he turned to me and heard my cry. He lifted me out of the slimy pit, out of the mud and mire; he set my feet on a rock and gave me a firm place to stand.
(Psalm 40:1-2, NIV)

Write your featured month verse here. Dissect the verse and re-write it using your own words. Doodle the verse. Print it. Repeat it as often as possible.

_____

_____

_____

_____

_____

_____

_____

_____

_____

_____

_____

_____

_____

_____

_____

✳ *Personal* ✳

My Thanksgiving... _____
_____
_____

My Repentance... _____
_____
_____

My Needs... _____
_____
_____

My Worries... _____
_____
_____

My Desires... _____
_____
_____

Who I need to forgive... _____
_____
_____

✳ *My Family* ✳

Family Name: _____

Concern: _____

Date Answered: _____

Family Name: _____

Concern: _____

Date Answered: _____

Family Name: _____

Concern: _____

Date Answered: _____

Family Name: _____

Concern: _____

Date Answered: _____

Family Name: _____

Concern: _____

Date Answered: _____

Family Name: _____

Concern: _____

Date Answered: _____

Family Name: _____

Concern: _____

Date Answered: _____

Family Name: _____

Concern: _____

Date Answered: _____

Family Name: _____

Concern: _____

Date Answered: _____

Family Name: _____

Concern: _____

Date Answered: _____

✳ *My Friends* ✳

Friend's Name: _____   Friend's Name: _____

Concern: _____   Concern: _____

Date Answered: _____   Date Answered: _____

Friend's Name: _____   Friend's Name: _____

Concern: _____   Concern: _____

Date Answered: _____   Date Answered: _____

Friend's Name: _____   Friend's Name: _____

Concern: _____   Concern: _____

Date Answered: _____   Date Answered: _____

Friend's Name: _____   Friend's Name: _____

Concern: _____   Concern: _____

Date Answered: _____   Date Answered: _____

Friend's Name: _____   Friend's Name: _____

Concern: _____   Concern: _____

Date Answered: _____   Date Answered: _____

✳ Prayers Requested by Others ✳

Name: _____   Name: _____

Concern: _____   Concern: _____

Date Answered: _____   Date Answered: _____

Name: _____   Name: _____

Concern: _____   Concern: _____

Date Answered: _____   Date Answered: _____

Name: _____   Name: _____

Concern: _____   Concern: _____

Date Answered: _____   Date Answered: _____

Name: _____   Name: _____

Concern: _____   Concern: _____

Date Answered: _____   Date Answered: _____

Name: _____   Name: _____

Concern: _____   Concern: _____

Date Answered: _____   Date Answered: _____

✴ Scribble your thoughts... ✴

He set my feet on a Rock & gave me a firm place to stand!

October, 20___

During this month, do your best to memorize this verse.

The thief comes only to steal and kill and destroy.
I have come that they may have life
and have it to the full.
(John 10:10, NIV)

Write your featured month verse here. Dissect the verse and re-write it using your own words. Doodle the verse. Print it. Repeat it as often as possible.

_____

_____

_____

_____

_____

_____

_____

_____

_____

_____

_____

_____

_____

_____

_____

_____

✴ *Personal* ✴

My Thanksgiving... _____
_____
_____

My Repentance... _____
_____
_____

My Needs... _____
_____
_____

My Worries... _____
_____
_____

My Desires... _____
_____
_____

Who I need to forgive... _____
_____
_____

✳ *My Family* ✳

Family Name: _____

Concern: _____

Date Answered: _____

Family Name: _____

Concern: _____

Date Answered: _____

Family Name: _____

Concern: _____

Date Answered: _____

Family Name: _____

Concern: _____

Date Answered: _____

Family Name: _____

Concern: _____

Date Answered: _____

Family Name: _____

Concern: _____

Date Answered: _____

Family Name: _____

Concern: _____

Date Answered: _____

Family Name: _____

Concern: _____

Date Answered: _____

Family Name: _____

Concern: _____

Date Answered: _____

Family Name: _____

Concern: _____

Date Answered: _____

✳ *My Friends* ✳

Friend's Name: _____   Friend's Name: _____

Concern: _____   Concern: _____

Date Answered: _____   Date Answered: _____

Friend's Name: _____   Friend's Name: _____

Concern: _____   Concern: _____

Date Answered: _____   Date Answered: _____

Friend's Name: _____   Friend's Name: _____

Concern: _____   Concern: _____

Date Answered: _____   Date Answered: _____

Friend's Name: _____   Friend's Name: _____

Concern: _____   Concern: _____

Date Answered: _____   Date Answered: _____

Friend's Name: _____   Friend's Name: _____

Concern: _____   Concern: _____

Date Answered: _____   Date Answered: _____

✳ Prayers Requested by Others ✳

Name: _____

Concern: _____

Date Answered: _____

Name: _____

Concern: _____

Date Answered: _____

Name: _____

Concern: _____

Date Answered: _____

Name: _____

Concern: _____

Date Answered: _____

Name: _____

Concern: _____

Date Answered: _____

Name: _____

Concern: _____

Date Answered: _____

Name: _____

Concern: _____

Date Answered: _____

Name: _____

Concern: _____

Date Answered: _____

Name: _____

Concern: _____

Date Answered: _____

Name: _____

Concern: _____

Date Answered: _____

✻ *Scribble your thoughts…* ✻

The devil destroys! Jesus came to give LIFE!

November, 20__ __

During this month, do your best to memorize this verse.

Because the Sovereign Lord helps me,
I will not be disgraced.
Therefore have I set my face like flint,
and I know I will not be put to shame.
(Isaiah 50: 7, NIV)

Write your featured month verse here. Dissect the verse and re-write it using your own words. Doodle the verse. Print it. Repeat it as often as possible.

_____

_____

_____

_____

_____

_____

_____

_____

_____

_____

_____

_____

_____

_____

_____

✳ *Personal* ✳

My Thanksgiving... _____

_____

_____

My Repentance... _____

_____

_____

My Needs... _____

_____

_____

My Worries... _____

_____

_____

My Desires... _____

_____

_____

Who I need to forgive... _____

_____

_____

✳ *My Family* ✳

Family Name: _____   Family Name: _____

Concern: _____   Concern: _____

Date Answered: _____   Date Answered: _____

Family Name: _____   Family Name: _____

Concern: _____   Concern: _____

Date Answered: _____   Date Answered: _____

Family Name: _____   Family Name: _____

Concern: _____   Concern: _____

Date Answered: _____   Date Answered: _____

Family Name: _____   Family Name: _____

Concern: _____   Concern: _____

Date Answered: _____   Date Answered: _____

Family Name: _____   Family Name: _____

Concern: _____   Concern: _____

Date Answered: _____   Date Answered: _____

✳ My Friends ✳

Friend's Name: _____

Concern: _____

Date Answered: _____

Friend's Name: _____

Concern: _____

Date Answered: _____

Friend's Name: _____

Concern: _____

Date Answered: _____

Friend's Name: _____

Concern: _____

Date Answered: _____

Friend's Name: _____

Concern: _____

Date Answered: _____

Friend's Name: _____

Concern: _____

Date Answered: _____

Friend's Name: _____

Concern: _____

Date Answered: _____

Friend's Name: _____

Concern: _____

Date Answered: _____

Friend's Name: _____

Concern: _____

Date Answered: _____

Friend's Name: _____

Concern: _____

Date Answered: _____

✳ *Prayers Requested by Others* ✳

Name: _____   Name: _____

Concern: _____   Concern: _____

Date Answered: _____   Date Answered: _____

Name: _____   Name: _____

Concern: _____   Concern: _____

Date Answered: _____   Date Answered: _____

Name: _____   Name: _____

Concern: _____   Concern: _____

Date Answered: _____   Date Answered: _____

Name: _____   Name: _____

Concern: _____   Concern: _____

Date Answered: _____   Date Answered: _____

Name: _____   Name: _____

Concern: _____   Concern: _____

Date Answered: _____   Date Answered: _____

✶ *Scribble your thoughts...* ✶

I have set my face like flint! I will not be ashamed!

December, 20_ _ _

During this month, do your best to memorize this verse.

*To him who is able to keep you from stumbling
and to present you before his glorious presence
without fault and with great joy –
to the only God our Savior be glory, majesty, power
and authority, through Jesus Christ our Lord,
before all ages, now and forevermore! Amen
(Jude 24-25, NIV)*

Write your featured month verse here. Dissect the verse and re-write it using your own words. Doodle the verse. Print it. Repeat it as often as possible.

_____
_____
_____
_____
_____
_____
_____
_____
_____
_____
_____
_____
_____
_____
_____
_____

✳ *Personal* ✳

My Thanksgiving... _____
_____
_____

My Repentance... _____
_____
_____

My Needs... _____
_____
_____

My Worries... _____
_____
_____

My Desires... _____
_____
_____

Who I need to forgive... _____
_____
_____

✴ My Family ✴

Family Name: _____

Concern: _____

Date Answered: _____

Family Name: _____

Concern: _____

Date Answered: _____

Family Name: _____

Concern: _____

Date Answered: _____

Family Name: _____

Concern: _____

Date Answered: _____

Family Name: _____

Concern: _____

Date Answered: _____

Family Name: _____

Concern: _____

Date Answered: _____

Family Name: _____

Concern: _____

Date Answered: _____

Family Name: _____

Concern: _____

Date Answered: _____

Family Name: _____

Concern: _____

Date Answered: _____

Family Name: _____

Concern: _____

Date Answered: _____

✳ My Friends ✳

Friend's Name: _____

Concern: _____

Date Answered: _____

Friend's Name: _____

Concern: _____

Date Answered: _____

Friend's Name: _____

Concern: _____

Date Answered: _____

Friend's Name: _____

Concern: _____

Date Answered: _____

Friend's Name: _____

Concern: _____

Date Answered: _____

Friend's Name: _____

Concern: _____

Date Answered: _____

Friend's Name: _____

Concern: _____

Date Answered: _____

Friend's Name: _____

Concern: _____

Date Answered: _____

Friend's Name: _____

Concern: _____

Date Answered: _____

Friend's Name: _____

Concern: _____

Date Answered: _____

✳ Prayers Requested by Others ✳

Name: _____   Name: _____

Concern: _____   Concern: _____

Date Answered: _____   Date Answered: _____

Name: _____   Name: _____

Concern: _____   Concern: _____

Date Answered: _____   Date Answered: _____

Name: _____   Name: _____

Concern: _____   Concern: _____

Date Answered: _____   Date Answered: _____

Name: _____   Name: _____

Concern: _____   Concern: _____

Date Answered: _____   Date Answered: _____

Name: _____   Name: _____

Concern: _____   Concern: _____

Date Answered: _____   Date Answered: _____

✳ *Scribble your thoughts...* ✳

To Him,
who is able!

✳ *Important Thoughts and Notes* ✳

To experience an original Broadway-style production by Martin & Clark visit the NarroWay Theatre just outside of Charlotte NC at 3327 Hwy. 51, Fort Mill SC. Find NarroWay online at narroway.net or request information by phone at 803.802.2300.

Additional works by Martin & Clark available at narroway.net and martinandclark.com.

Made in the USA
Columbia, SC
27 November 2023

26812989R00057